EPILEPSY AND DEPRESSION

# WEB WAS WOVEN

SONNY CHASE

authorHOUSE®

*AuthorHouse™*
*1663 Liberty Drive*
*Bloomington, IN 47403*
*www.authorhouse.com*
*Phone: 1 (800) 839-8640*



*Published by AuthorHouse 08/06/2018*

*ISBN: 978-1-5462-5404-1 (sc)*
*ISBN: 978-1-5462-5403-4 (e)*

*Library of Congress Control Number: 2018909193*

*Print information available on the last page.*



*This book is printed on acid-free paper.*

# Contents

# Beginning of it all

Hello, my name is Sonny Chase, I am writing this book for you and families whose lives have been, or are about to be, transformed by epilepsy.

It is my sincerest hope that by sharing my personal experiences growing up with epilepsy and then, finally undergoing brain surgery to control it, you will feel you are not alone, and more importantly, you will realize there is hope that you or your loved one, can overcome this condition. I welcome any questions or feedback you might have for me, which you can e-mail at webwaswoven@sonnychase.org.

I hope my story will make you smile and comfort you during this challenging time.

I was born in 1967 in a suburban city called Coon Rapids, Minnesota, located on the Mississippi River just 20 miles north of the Twin Cities. I arrived two months earlier than expected, weighing only 4 ½ pounds. The doctors kept me in the hospital for two weeks to gain more weight before my parents were allowed to bring me home.

Aside from being born prematurely, the first 14 months of my life were relatively uneventful. But this would all change come Christmas 1968. My father, Danny, was out enjoying an evening cup of coffee with his close friend Ray, the drummer of his rock and roll band. But while I was at home with my mom, whose real name is Lynnette, but everyone calls her "Nettie."

My mother said she had spent the earlier part of the day tending to me, as I was sick with a fever. Although she says my temperature was high. We do not know exactly how high it was at the time because she did not have a thermometer.

Being teenage parents, they had to get by on the single income of my 19-year-old father because my mom was still in high school. My mother did her best to cool me down by gently pressing my head and face with cold, wet washcloths.

Finally, feeling both exhausted, yet satisfied that she had reduced my temperature, she rocked me to sleep and laid me back down into my crib before crawling into her own bed getting some much-needed rest.

Two hours later she awoke to the sound of the Christmas tree toppling over. This was strange, she thought. Being I had began walking at the age of six months, she had leaned the tree up against the wall of the trailer house in order to prevent me from getting into trouble with it.

As she walked past my crib to check on the tree, she discovered what had to be a new mother's nightmare, her baby boy's helpless little body lying in the crib, trembling, with his eyes rolling into the back of his head.

It turned out I was having convulsions and I had shaken my crib hard enough to knock the wall upon which that Christmas tree was leaning, causing the tree to fall over.

My mom has always said that the sound of that tree falling saved my life that night, because had I laid there convulsing much longer, it could have caused irreversible brain damage, or worse, it could have killed me.

Making matters worse, it was close to midnight, my parents did not have a telephone back then, and my father had their only vehicle, so my mother was stuck in the trailer park with me until my father came home, which was, thank goodness, just a few minutes later.

With me still twitching in her arms, my mother was waiting by the door when my father walked in. She told him they needed to rush me to the hospital as quickly as possible.

Together they sped off to the hospital by this time my poor 17-year-old mother was panicking.

Upon arriving to the hospital, I was still twitching in my mother's arms. When she told the doctors and nurses she found me convulsing and that I had had a fever all day.

They immediately took me from my mother's arms and rushed me into a separate room. The nurse told my mother she was just going to check my temperature. Then shortly after, the nurse returned to inform my mother that they had given me an injection of Phenobarbital, a strong barbiturate commonly used to treat seizures or decades ago, anxiety.

My young, exhausted mother felt scared, alone, and confused. She was upset they did not give her the opportunity to ask questions about or altogether refuse the drug on my behalf.

And as if that weren't bad enough, they also informed my mother that after giving the injection, my little body suddenly became limp, and the staff noticed the entire side of my body was no longer responsive.

The doctors said they were not sure whether the paralysis was a side effect of the Phenobarbital, the needle hitting a nerve, or a result of the convulsion, itself.

My mother said she was told years later by our trusted family physician that because my little body was still twitching, making it impossible to hold me still, it was possible the needle hit a nerve, and for that reason he would have never injected a convulsing baby the way they did.

Later that evening they performed a spinal tap on me, also known as a lumbar puncture, or LP, which is commonly done in cases where convulsions coexist with a high fever in order to rule out bacterial meningitis, but my results came back negative.

The doctors decided to admit me and keep me under observation for a week. My parents were sad to go home without me once again.

Four months later, I would have my first official seizure, but because my mother was not there, not much was being done about it at the time.

It was a hot summer day and I was at my grandmother's house. She told my mother that I had a strange expression on my face and I appeared to be shivering, but when she asked me if I was cold, I did not respond, until a few minutes later. In my mom's words, "this was the beginning of everything."

## The 1970’s

In 1970, at the age of 3, my parents noticed me daydreaming on occasion, but nobody really thought much of it at the time.

I was also beginning to experience what is known as seizure auras, which typically occur up to one minute before the onset of a seizure and can range from mild sensory interferences to full blown hallucinations.

My auras seemed to be triggered by the loud, rhythmic sounds of airplanes and trains and the odor of gasoline and rubber.

1971 was a very special time for me. Not only because my mother had my sister, CheraLynn (“Chera”), but because my father, (who looked like the young Elvis) and was the lead singer and guitarist of his rock and roll band.) and also with his great friend my Godfather, Jon, they took me down to the Twin Cities to see Elvis Presley in concert.

During the concert my dad and I were excited watching one of Elvis’ scarves land on a security guard, and witness all of the ladies in the audience attack him for it.

After seeing this, my mom says I began to build my own stages around the house and throw scarves to the women in my pretend audiences, just like Elvis did.

The next milestone in my life with epilepsy occurred in 1976, the time my mother and I had to stay up all night long in preparation for my first EEG, the doctors wanted me to sleep through the procedure. (My EEG was a test that measures and records my electrical activity of my brain using special sensors, or electrodes, attached to little plates that were pasted onto my head and are then hooked up by wires to a huge computer............. I was 9 years old at the time. My results showed there were no focal abnormalities, meaning there were no specific areas of my brain that showed anything wrong. Yet, signs of seizures were still observed in my behavior.

Whenever I had a seizure, I would tell my mom that I was cold. I suppose, being so young, I had no other way to explain what I was feeling.

The type of seizures I was having were called focal seizures, also known as partial seizures or localized seizures, which are seizures that affected, at least initially, only one hemisphere.

The neurologists started me on an anti-seizure medication called Dilantin, which was the first of many medications to come. With this I had to take folic acid supplements in order to counteract the swelling of my gums, a well-known, and unfortunate, side effect of the drug that can make your gums tender and bleed.

After nine years of tests and seeing doctors, I was finally diagnosed with epilepsy. My parents and teachers began to notice a gradual change in my personality, memory, and other issues affected by the medications. And I was still having seizures.

For the most part, I had a lot of fun in my childhood years playing with my neighborhood friends.

In the winter months we would walk down to the ice rink to play hockey then in the summer months I used to walk down to the neighborhood swimming pool with my friends and little sister. It was so much fun back in the seventies.

My friends and I would either ride our bikes or walk three blocks from home, goofing around and playing the whole way there. Working up a sweat made the swimming even that much better!

One particular summer day, while my friends and I were jumping into the deep end of the Olympic-style swimming pool.

I felt a seizure aura coming on and grew scared, but fortunately it went away quickly. I worried about what I should do. My friends just told me to rest for a little bit and never made a big deal out of it. Shortly after, I was back in action again.

But this sense of fear and uncertainty would return more and more as I got older. In elementary and junior high school, the classroom was a very stressful place for me.

My medications made it difficult for me to memorize my multiplication tables and spelling words, getting me in trouble for "not applying myself" or taking my schoolwork seriously.

I was also always worried about having seizures and getting hurt or made fun of by the other kids—although I do want to point out that my good friends were always there for me.

I can still remember one time very clearly (and painfully) that occurred while sitting in my desk in a very quiet classroom taking a history test. Without warning, my right arm went out, sending all of my schoolbooks crashing down onto the hard tile floor below. If that were not embarrassing enough, I also loudly mumbled words that made no sense to anyone at all… all of this during a test I had been dwelling on for a week straight.

This and similar episodes taught my family that stress and fatigue were strong triggers for my seizures. This was a catch-22 for me, though, because I was stressing out about having the seizures in the first place! Plus, the medication made my memory bad, so I would forget to take my pills on time—another perfect recipe for a seizure, we learned.

So being at school was definitely not easy for me. Sometimes I wonder how I would have done in school if not for my epilepsy…

From controlling the time I went to bed, to controlling the type of food I was allowed to eat, the remainder of my adolescent years were spent devoting my life to managing my epilepsy.

My doctors experimented with my medications, all of which having different side effects but none of them really working, and my parents experimented with my daily routine, such as enforcing a strict sleep regimen and forcing me to try the latest sugar-free but to no avail.

## Beginning of adulthood

In the early to mid-eighties, my late teens, I was still visiting my neurologist and undergoing various types of tests. We kept our fingers crossed each time, hoping we would find something, anything, to explain the cause of my seizures.

Finally, a calcium deposit began to appear on my MRI tests.

I was told the deposits were due to a disease called Mesial Temporal Sclerosis, or MTS, which is a scarring in the inner portions of the temporal lobe, the parts of the brain located just underneath the temples.

Uncontrolled seizures were thought to be the cause of this scar tissue forming. Learning more about what was happening inside my head felt good, but back then we were told not much could be done about it without risking further brain damage.

The neurologist did help with the medications, however. He switched me from Dilantin to Tegretol, which is used for treating chronic nerve pain as well as seizures. I was thrilled to get off from Dilantin, because after using it for four years my gums were getting puffy. But still, these drugs weren't cheap, especially considering I would not get my first health insurance for another ten years.

I remember there were times my mother had to choose between buying groceries for us and buying my medication. This made me feel guilty and curse my epilepsy even more, because I did not like seeing my mother upset.

Also at this time, like most teenagers, I wanted so badly to get my driver's license, but my epilepsy did not allow me to. As a young guy who was really into dirt biking and mechanically working on engines, this was especially hard on me.

As a result, I felt left out watching all of my friends get their licenses, picking up their girlfriends, and driving around having fun without needing their parents or older siblings to drive them. I didn't feel as independent as they did. I still needed someone to drop me off and come get me wherever I went either that or ride the city bus, which was even more embarrassing.

I actually rode my bike, even in the cold Minnesota winters! Looking back, I think this was one of the first major forks in the road between my peers and me growing up. For all of my friends, this was their "coming of age," so to speak, their "rite of passage," the start of their new exciting journey into manhood. I was feeling left behind, kind of depressed, I guess, but not yet to a level of concern.

As I got older, I had more and more seizures away from my parents and out in public, and sometimes this caused a scene. Once, while shopping at a Target store with a friend, my sister, and her friend, we were all in the music section looking at vinyl LP's and cassette tapes.

My sister said she noticed the expression on my face change, my right arm stiffen up, and my right hand begin clenching and opening repeatedly, all telltale signs I was about to have a seizure. Before she could reach for me, she saw me fall over in slow motion, just like a tall tree that had just been cut at the base.

I fell down face first onto the hard, tile floor with my arms hanging limply at my sides—BAM! It was awful to watch, and even worse to hear. My sister ran to me to prop up my head and hold my hand, telling me I was going to be okay (she never panicked, she had grown up watching me have seizures her whole life).

Customers and store employees had witnessed the fall and immediately called an ambulance to come get me. My sister tried to tell them I had epilepsy and I was going to be okay, but they did not listen to her. There I was, my day cut short, headed back to the hospital with a big ambulance bill to pay.

After graduating in 1986, I decided to get away from everything and take an adventure that did not require driving or watching my friends drive.

I flew up to British Columbia to visit my grandparents and work on their lodge in the majestic Northern Rocky

Mountains. Along the cold, swiftly moving Coal River, just three and a half hours below the Alaskan border. The trip was breathtaking. I had a blast taking pictures of the moose, ravens, bears, and other amazing wildlife definitely things I didn't see back home in Minnesota!

I also enjoyed snowmobiling in the mountains with my uncles. The trip was great experience, that is, until I had a seizure doing something as mundane as taking out the trash. I fell right onto the red-hot burn barrel, severely burning the back of my right hand. The scar is a permanent reminder of that day and my epilepsy.

Having epilepsy continued to be both expensive and painful for me. In 1988 I was back home, working the night shift at a Mobile Gas Station (it was the only job I could take at the time, because I was able to arrange a ride to and from work with a coworker—yet another life-altering incident of my epilepsy).

As a 24-year- old otherwise healthy young man, working those hours wasn't that big of a deal for me that is until one night in October, when I had a seizure while cleaning up the car repair garage.

It was usually the responsibility of the mechanics to clean this part of the station, but because the mechanic was running late that night, I offered to take care of it during my shift.

Later that night, with a lack of sleep, I began to feel a seizure aura, which meant a seizure was eminent. I managed to make it over to the telephone and quickly called my father, but I completely collapsed after hanging up, falling into the transmission stand that fell on top of me as I hit the concrete floor.

A customer entered the station sometime afterwards and found me lying there. He called for an ambulance and I ended up spending the night in the hospital with a concussion.

Like the driver's license, this experience made me feel less like a man. To me, that night meant I could not even be left alone to work at a gas station, an entry-level job. First my school, then my social life, and now my job--what kind of life was in store for me with my epilepsy? I was feeling alone and getting more depressed

## Close calls

In 1992 I was really happy to have found a job in carpentry that did not require me to drive. Unlike the gas station job, I loved working outside and being able to visit with my coworkers.

I've also always liked working with my hands and learning to use new tools and build new things. I was really excited about this job. The night before, I would pack my lunch, the way my father always did. And in the mornings, I couldn't wait to get up and put on my work boots and tool belt.

I hoped this job would last, and I could make a career out of it until my body starts to change its mind. I figured that even if I couldn't drive, I would figure out how to still make enough money to buy or build my own house someday, get married, and raise a family all of the things men are supposed to be able to do.

But again, as with my past experiences, the job went well for a while until I had seizure. On Thanksgiving day the company had its employees work until noon to finish a job, and at eleven o'clock they sent me up onto the roof to quickly remove some boards so we could all go home to our families and celebrate the holiday.

As I climbed the ladder, I began to feel another aura coming on. Oh no! My boss didn't know about my epilepsy and I didn't want him to, so I kept climbing. (This was a terrible decision I would make more than once in my lifetime with tragic consequences.)

Once I was up there, I grabbed hold of the chimney for a second, bracing myself as I determined what to do next.

There was so much at stake with this job, I could not afford to lose it. The next thing I remembered was being put into a car and being raced to the nearest hospital. I was told later that I had fallen two stories and landed face down, on my hands and knees.

This time I was injured very badly, but the doctors said it would have been much worse were it not for the fact I was unconscious and unable to brace myself for the impact.

Had I braced myself, they said, I would have surely shattered my arms and legs. It goes without saying that the carpentry job was gone.

Jobless and renting my fathers basement apartment, where there is no public transportation, I was isolated and depressed. I struggled for two years to find consistant work after the roof incident. Finally, in 1994, I managed to get hired at a large metal factory.

It wasn't the best job in the world, the air was hot and smoky, but by then I was desperate to get any kind of work I could, also, this one offered benefits!

In 1995 I received health insurance for the very first time in my entire life, which was a tremendous relief with all of my expensive medications, mounting medical bills, and the stress it had put on my family.

I quickly made an appointment at the hospital and got to meet a new Epileptologist. She suggested another EEG so she could see what was going on. I really thought she was a wonderful specialist who genuinely wanted the very best for me.

She changed my medication to Felbatol, a brand name for felbamate. I had to take regular blood tests while I was on this medicine to make sure my liver was okay.

I decided to eventually stop using this drug, though, because I found out later that my epilepsy was a preexisting condition, and my new insurance wouldn't cover it or the blood tests.

Besides, I noticed it was making me very edgy and irritable. One time, while out shopping with my father, some kids gave us the finger for some reason and I was ready to go fight them, all by myself. I was pretty riled up, but my dad pulled me back and talked me back down. That was the Felbatol.

Unfortunately, without the insurance the testing also had to stop because I could not afford it.

I worked at that job for three years. Over that period of time I managed to arrange transportation from coworkers and family members and I did disclose my epilepsy to my employers.

They were supportive, which was nice. But despite the inconvenience of continuing to take massive doses of strong, expensive psychotropic medications, all with unwanted side effects, it was not long before it happened, even at this job. I ended up having three seizures while working there.

The first seizure happened with only one other coworker there to see it. Embarrassed and afraid of losing my job, I asked him not to tell anyone. He kept our secret he was pretty supportive. Deep down, though, I hated that my epilepsy had turned me into a liar.

I felt guilty keeping secrets from my employers, who were so supportive of me. So I had another seizure while driving a forklift. I was picking up a load of heavy sheet metal when all of a sudden I felt an aura coming on. This one was terrifying, because my foot got stuck holding the gas pedal down to the floor!

Fortunately, I had the where withal to reach down and bump the shifting lever into neutral, so all it did was rev up the engine until my coworker ran over and turn the motor off. I was lucky that the place was really loud with machines clanking and motors running, so only a few people heard the commotion.

That was a close call, though. I didn't drive the forklift anymore after that.

My third and final seizure at that job occurred in the lunchroom area. Just like at the Target store, I fell and hit my head on the hard concrete floor (it's amazing how many head injuries I've suffered as a result of my epilepsy).

This time, instead of having a focal seizure, I had a grand mal seizure, the type that causes complete unconsciousness.

Although my head hurt, I'd have to say the embarrassment was the worst part of it, the same as it had been in school.

In school, relationships, and work, it seemed no matter which direction I turned, my epilepsy stood in the way as a barrier I could not overcome. It's a wonder I never gave up… but I was definitely becoming more depressed.

In 1996, money issues were causing serious tension with my father. After talking it over with my sister, Chera, she sent me a Greyhound bus ticket to come work on her horse ranch in California.

I packed my things and jumped on a bus to begin another journey. I waited for the bus to show up in St. Paul, Mn and while waiting for the bus, It was interesting seeing all the different people transferring from one bus to another.

I finally boarded the bus and started going north towards northern Minnesota and then heading west through ND, Montana, Idaho and Washington. On that journey I met a lot of different people, their life changing situations or just traveling to see family or like me, a journey.

While traveling through North Dakota it was kind of boring but most of it was late evening anyway. Montana was very beautiful with the mountain ranges and even part of Yellowstone national park while going through Idaho. While going through Idaho we stopped in another pickup location and a large lady entered the bus heading for the rear seat.

Because of her size it was the most comfortable place for her. When we reached Washington and took off south going through Oregon she had not moved for a while.

The bus pulled over a little later and ended up getting in a different bus because she had passed away a while back. A young lady I talked to had family issues and left home to move to southern California to start over. You start getting a different look on life when you get to hear others with issues they also have to deal with.

Back now to my sister, she lived and still lives, in the small, rural, old-western town of Weed, California, which is in the Siskiyou Mountains at the base of the inspiring, snowcapped Mt. Shasta just 40 minutes south of the Oregon border.

Chera left Minnesota back in 1991 to work for her now-husband, Mustafa, managing his herd of 300 Arabian horses, which are bred for racing and showing (and even flown on airplanes to compete in horse shows worldwide!).

The ranch consisted of close to 800 acres and backed up into Federal land containing the world famous Pacific Crest Trail, which people hike and ride horses from Mexico to Canada without having to open a single gate.

The fresh, clean mountain air, the ranch, its animals, and being with my sister and her husband were all therapeutic for me. I enjoyed going out to feed the horses each morning and driving the ranch truck up into the mountains to cut firewood for the potbelly stove in the living room.

My sweetest memories involve a small river flowing through the entire length of the ranch known as the "China Ditch".

It was built by Chinese slaves hundreds of years ago to deliver snow melting from the mountain tops 90 miles to irrigate local farms. Lucky for me, upriver from the ranch is the local fish hatchery, where they grow Rainbow and German Brown Trout.

Those fish that detoured from Shasta River into the China Ditch ended up in the ranch, some even ended up falling into the springs and lakes of the ranch by way of irrigation ditches.

So every night, after a hard day's work putting up barns and taking down old barbed wire fences, I grabbed my fishing pole and tackle box and headed out to the China Ditch.

I swung my net back and forth in front of my legs as I walked through the meadows, catching loads of grasshoppers for bait as they jumped up in front of my feet. I would stay out there until dark, experimenting with different ways to catch the trout, even learning to fly fish.

The water was not very deep and the trout were real spooky, so I eventually figured out to stand further away and behind a giant Ponderosa Pine tree, so they couldn't see me as I casted out. They were really good eating.

Of course, my epilepsy came with me to California, along with all its physical and emotional baggage. I had seizures there, some they knew about and some they didn't. Mustafa used to worry about me, always catastrophizing when I didn't come in from fishing just after sunset that I had had a seizure and fallen into the China Ditch, drowning.

One night I found him out there walking along the China Ditch in the dark with a flashlight, calling my name. He was a great guy who really cared about me and still does.

But one day I would have a seizure and it would cause damage to the property and the ranch truck. Mustafa happened to be down in the Bay Area at the time (he was often tending to business at their house in the Santa Cruz Mountains or their mental health facility for people with schizophrenia in downtown San Jose).

Chera and I were preparing the barn and a group of horses for a potential buyer who was flying in from Hollywood the following week. We were rushing to get things cleaned up, so she took a risk and let me use the ranch truck to drag the horse arena.

She made me promise that I would stop the truck and get out if I felt a seizure coming on. She pointed out where she wanted me to go and then went back inside the barn to groom horses.

She said she heard a big crash and all of the horses in the barn spooked, so she ran outside to find me in the truck with the truck doing a handstand, pointing nose-down into an irrigation ditch.

She looked behind the truck and saw a trail of destruction… I had driven the truck through the wooden arena fence, breaking the wooden post and several rails, through the grass, a wire fence, and then up an embankment and into the ditch.

The hood and bumper of the truck were dented and the windshield was cracked.

I had a bloody gash on my nose and forehead from hitting the hard, old-fashioned steering wheel upon impact. Chera didn't know what to say, she was worried about me but she was also confused as to why I would not keep my promise to stop the truck and get out. All I could tell her was that I did feel the aura, but I did not know why I didn't stop the truck and get out of it.

She quickly drove us to the hardware store to buy supplies to fix the damage. I remember working so fast, we even got a neighbor to help us bury a new post into the ground, surround it with concrete, attach new rails to it, and then paint all of it to match the rest of the fence.

We even pulled most of the dents out of the truck using the bucket of the excavator and a sledgehammer. Mustafa and the client arrived the day after, and the horse showing went off without a hitch.

Chera and I were not going to tell Mustafa about it, because we didn't want him to get mad or worry about me, but he noticed the crack in the windshield and we eventually had to tell him the whole story. I felt bad about that and hated my epilepsy even more for making me do it.

There were many more incidents like this… Perhaps those can be material for my next book?

I ended up heading home shortly after. Finding a new job and moving on for an unknown future.

# A devastating Three months

After a few years back home, working a new job in Fridley, Mn I met up with my high school sweatheart Dawn Anderson from back in 1984 – 1986. In September of the year 2000 I moved to Appleton, to be with Dawn, (after her divorce) and her three children.

After finally going a year without a seizure, due to a new medication called Neurontin, also a nerve pain medication, I was finally able to get my driver's license— this was something to celebrate!

It was a huge confidence-builder for me to finally be able to sustain what felt like a more normal life. Of course, I had to find a job so I could bring home an income for the family.

After a few weeks of searching, I found a new job in Green Bay working at a metal plating factory with a 45-minute commute.

What a feeling; to finally be driving! It was incredible I felt so independent. I was finally becoming the man I had almost given up dreaming I'd become. After working there for several weeks I ended up coming down with the flu and was forced to stay home for four days.

I got so tired of just lying around at home and couldn't stand one more day of it, so I decided to at least show up for work the next day, even if only to be told to turn right back around and go home. (This would turn out to be yet another poor decision.

So I pulled myself out of bed the next morning and drove myself to work…or, at least that was what I intended to do. Pulling out of the driveway, I had no idea what was about to happen.

The truth is, I had been under so much stress that past week, thinking about my finances, my relationship with my father and settling into a new household, in a new state, that was filled with the daily bustle of three kids (whom I love dearly, by the way).

And I had also been vomiting those past few days, which made me tired and dehydrated and, something I would realize after the fact, also caused the level of medication in my blood to drop dangerously low. Just five minutes after leaving the house, while entering into heavy traffic, I felt a seizure aura coming on.

Panicking, I wondered if I should try to pull over as quickly as possible or try to fight it (Wich has never worked for me) And that's as far as it went.

As I slowly started coming back to consciousness, I heard a man in a large SUV yelling from across the road. I also noticed that the hood of my car was twisted with a cloud of steam rising up from underneath. I closed my eyes and prayed to God that I was dreaming. Hoping that it would all go away. But it didn't.

Next I could hear the police sirens in the distance, faded at first, but then becoming louder and louder as it got closer. I was scared, because I wasn't even myself, yet.

Dawn arrived after a friend of ours called her, explaining she was in the same bunch of traffic I was in and she'd just seen what happened. Dawn was both angry and scared at the same time, and, of course, I couldn't blame her.

Just hours after the accident, Dawn and I had a long talk, and together we made the decision (this time a wise decision) that I would surrender my license and not drive anymore, which meant I probably wouldn't be able to work, anymore, either.

Instead, I would become a stay-at-home father for my stepdaughter, Kaleigh. Thank goodness Dawn was making a high enough income that we had the luxury to make such a drastic decision otherwise, I don't know what we would have done. I was torn between feeling happy to have a partner who accepted my epilepsy, but sad that my epilepsy once again prevented me from being the man I wanted to be for her.

A couple of months later, February 3rd 2001, Dawn and I had our wedding. It was a crisp, freezing cold day in Minnesota.

There was already 8 inches of snow on the ground with more falling throughout the day, and the temperature was only 12° F, but felt like 2 below zero, with a bitter wind chill.

All bundled up, everyone was slipping and sliding on the icy sidewalk as they filed into the church one by one in their slick dress shoes. I remember keeping myself busy by entertaining Kaleigh, the little five-year-old daughter of my soon-to-be- wife.

Soon it was just us guys and the little kids out in the hallway. All of the ladies were busy in the dressing room putting on their gowns and doing their hair and makeup They were trying to make themselves even more beautiful than they already were.

I was a little tired from all of the preparations of a big church wedding, but I was also really excited. I had a lot on my mind that day. I was happy my father showed up and my sister flew in from California, but there was an underlying awkwardness in the air due to the merging of our four sets of parents, both sides of whom had divorced decades earlier.

Of course, aside from all of that, I had one more big concern bouncing around inside my head, and that was the fear of having a seizure during the ceremony while everything was quiet— just like that memorable, embarrassing day back in history class, when I had a seizure and knocked all of the books off my desk.

I didn't want my epilepsy to ruin our big day. My bride did not deserve that after all she went through to organize such a beautiful wedding.

Shortly after, and to my surprise, the girls came out of the dressing room looking even more beautiful than they did going in. By this time people were moving about, making last minute adjustments and finding seats for the guests.

While greeting the guests as they arrived, I began to feel seizure auras coming on, and my heart sunk. I prayed to God harder than ever before, asking him to let me get through the ceremony without having a seizure.

Now I was distracted with the countdown going on in the back of my head…

The big moment came, everyone was seated and the members of the wedding party were all in their places—the church was quiet.

I just dreaded what was about to happen next. Coincidentally, the pastor and almost all of the guests were well aware of my seizures, as most of our friends and family members had witnessed my seizures growing up.

With shear might, I was able to fight back the seizure until it came to the point when we were supposed to exchange our vows, and that's when it hit! My sister told me she could see the expression on my face start to go blank and my right hand begin making a fist, and she knew it was about to happen.

My father and my best man, a school buddy who had seen me go through many seizures over the years, immediately jumped up onto the altar, each one grabbing an arm and guiding me carefully down to the front pew, where I sat a few minutes to recover.

I slowly came back to a state of awareness and waited a few seconds to get my balance again before returning to the alter, where my beautiful almost-wife was waiting so lovingly and patiently. This time I was surrounded by a large group of people who deeply cared about me.

All of the awkwardness and nervousness was gone, and I could really feel the love in the room. Afterwards, my sister told me that my seizure did not ruin the wedding, but instead it made it more real. In a strange way, it brought everyone into the moment, a special moment we all experienced together and will never forget.

The rest of the ceremony went on without any hang-ups and I went to rest before the reception, which turned out to be a fabulous night.

My life changed for the better after that day. I knew I was in the right place with Dawn, the love of my life. One month later, we found out that Dawn would be having a baby. On September 6$^{th}$, 2001 our beautiful daughter, Riley, was born.

## Made a decision

In 2003 we moved to Detroit Lakes, in northern Minnesota to accommodate a job transfer for Dawn. We bought a nice house across the street from Little Floyd Lake, where we could use my fishing boat and raise our children in a wholesome community setting.

We became active in the local church—I even began teaching Bible school, counseling peers, and playing guitar in the church band. I enjoyed fixing things around the house, mowing the lawn, and helping our elderly neighbors with their landscaping, too.

I even set up a wood shop to build handmade electric guitars that I sold on the Internet. I was doing what I could to keep myself busy while Dawn was away at work.

Also during that time, because I was now Dawn's husband, I was finally able to get good health insurance through her work, I started seeing doctors over in North Dakota, but I didn't feel we were making any progress, because they were assigning my case to a new neurologist every year.

This meant starting from scratch, explaining my whole life's story over and over and dealing with fluctuations in my medications as each new doctor adjusted my medications as he or she saw fit. And, although I adored my new family and our new life together, it wasn't easy living out in the country with only one family member driving. So caring for the new little baby, especially with Dawn being both the mother and the breadwinner, who was forced to be on the road several days and nights each week.

I had to learn on-the-fly how to be a fulltime father to our new little daughter and work with neighbors to get rides or the things I needed from the stores while Dawn was out of town each week.

During those repetitive years the quality of my life definitely declined. I was becoming more and more stressed out, and by then we had no choice but to raise the levels of my medication higher and higher, worsening side effects such as sleepiness, irritability, poor memory, and confusion, basically making my life unbearable.

In 2011, I finally asked to have my case referred to a clinic in Blaine, MN, because I had to try something new. The first neurologist I saw in Blaine was the first one ever to admit to me that the severity of my condition was outside his scope of professional competence.

In a nutshell, he said he could combine different medications, which would only drug me up even further, but this would not improve the quality of my life in any way.

He referred me to an Epileptologist, which I found out was a neurologist who has acquired an expertise in seizures and seizure disorders, anticonvulsants etc. Their training typically ranges from one to several years through postgraduate work with a unique focus on epilepsy. They are typically consulted when epilepsy cases are not responding well to initial treatments, such as drugs.

I connected with the Epileptologist and resumed the extensive testing where I had left off back in 1995. It was refreshing.

The doctors explained to me that after all of those years of suffering. Brain surgery might actually be an option for me now—an idea that both intrigued and frightened the living daylights out of Dawn and I.

We found out that patients with epilepsy, whose seizures originate from the temporal lobe, have a high probability that their seizures will not be controlled with anti-seizure medications alone,

And that surgery for this type of epilepsy is well-established. But first we had to determine if I was even a candidate for the surgery. We packed up the car and drove down to twin cities to spend the next four days undergoing various tests.

First they performed an EEG, and an MRI on me, and then they used the results from those tests to create

MSI's, or Magnetic Source Images, which gave them spatial 3-D computer animated views, of my brain.

This allowed them to see the temporal scarring of my Mesial Temporal Sclerosis and how it was affecting the electrical activity in my brain. They used these images to formulate a strategy and serve as a visible guide during surgery.

The third exam they did with me was the WADA, named after Juhn Atsushi Wada, the Canadian neurologist who invented it, and it's typically administered by a neuropsychologist as a result of its required expertise in psychological measurements.

I think the purpose of the WADA is pretty straightforward, which is to find out what is happening in each hemisphere, or side, of my brain by shutting down the opposite hemisphere.

But the application of it was a little creepy to me. I will try not to get technical with this. First of all, they started out by inserting an intra catheter into my femoral artery, located in my groin, and then carefully pushed the catheter all the way up into each side of my brain, one hemisphere at a time.

And they had to do this while I was awake, because I had to answer questions during this test! Once the catheter reached one of my hemispheres, the doctor injected a drug called amobarbital.

The drug was injected into one hemisphere at a time—if the artery on the right side of my groin was injected, then the right side of my brain was inhibited and could not communicate with the left side.

The goal was to shut down any language and/or memory functions in one hemisphere in order to evaluate the language and/or memory functions in the other hemisphere. And see what there was for risks.

Lastly, the fourth test we did was the NPE, or neuropsychological evaluation. This was actually a collection of smaller verbal or action tests that helped my specialist understand how I thought, moved, behaved, talked, read, and "made decisions" (Decisions is my business name).

All in all, the tests took about six months and my medications were changed and adjusted accordingly. After all of that, the doctors surprised me with news… I qualified for surgery!

But now that brain surgery was a real possibility, the whole idea of it seemed scarier than it did before, back when I used to think it would never happen. Day and night, I bounced the risks and potential gains back and forth in my head like a Ping-Pong ball. Would I be doing the right thing if I went through with the surgery?

Here is a list of things I thought about just before surgery:

On the one hand, my family needed me to take care of them, because Dawn needed to be free to go to work so we could pay our bills and buy our food. If I were laid up, who would take care of the kids?

How long would I be in the hospital and then home recovering? Who would take care of me? Would there be any side effects to the surgery? Could I die on the table? What if I don't wake up?

What if I wake up, but I'm not the same person? What if I'm brain damaged and can't see or can't remember anything or anyone? Is it selfish for me to want this? How would this play out, would it even be possible?

I decided to call up our pastor and invite him over to the house to talk it over with us. I really liked him a lot. He was always very supportive of our family and me. He came over for coffee one afternoon and we had a heart to heart talk. In the end, he helped me to feel good about making my decision, no matter what that ended up being.

Dawn didn't push me either way, but I could tell, even without her saying, that she didn't think things were going to get any better on their own. We had gotten to the point that something had to be done, because even without the surgery I was dying a slow, agonizing death.

We realized we had no choice but to take the risk and vowed to hold one another's hand and walk through the journey together, one step at a time. We informed the doctors and loved ones and made all the necessary arrangements with family members to watch the kids while we were gone. All that was left was to count down the days.

March 2nd, 2011 would mark the beginning of a real rollercoaster ride for Dawn and I. Driving down to the hospital and staying in a hotel the night before, that morning Dawn and I entered the hospital for my surgery around 5:00 AM.

Before letting me go any further, they pulled a sample of my blood to perform the necessary pre-op blood tests. Our bubble burst when they informed us that my iron level was too low for me to have surgery.

What a letdown, especially after all of the emotional buildup and logistical hassle we went through to get there, such as Dawn taking off work and arranging for our mothers, who also had to take off work, to alternate staying up in our house in Detroit Lakes.

So, discouraged and with iron pills in hand, we ended up driving the four hours back home the same day.

I immediately started the supplements, changed my diet, and made appointments at the local clinic to get my iron checked. But week after week, it never did get (and stay) high enough.

An interesting discovery in my medical records at that time revealed that my iron level was also low when I had my convulsion at the age of 13-months-old.

With this information in mind, the surgeon made the decision that no matter what, I would have my surgery the following month. (I liked that decision!)

Surgery day was April 2nd. It was scary for Dawn and myself. We repeated all the steps we took the previous month, driving down and staying in a hotel the night before.

That morning we checked in real early (again) and were led down to the preparation area, where they had me strip out of my clothes and put on a hospital gown. I crawled up onto the bed and pulled the blankets up over me to keep warm. The blankets had a comforting effect, too, which felt good, because I was getting nervous.

The waiting was over, and I was amazed it was really going to happen this time, that the next time I put my clothes back on I would be a different person, and I had no idea who that person would be.

I couldn't help but notice I couldn't stop tapping my feet while waiting for everything to start. Soon the nurses came in to get me ready. I was relieved when they gave me some medication to relax me a little bit. Putting the IV into the back of my hand was difficult for some reason, they had to use warm towels to locate my veins (reality seemed to really set in once the wristband was on and my IV was in).

There was no going back now. I couldn't get it out of my head that my life, as I knew, that morning was going to be forever changed by the decision I made to have surgery.

## Here we go

Next, my brain surgeon, came into the room with her large coffee, all ready to go for the day. I really liked her a lot and felt safe just being around her. She always seemed so smart and confident and was always good at moving everything along smoothly.

She asked Dawn and I how we were doing and then asked me if I was ready for my big day. Nodding my head, I smiled and said, "I sure am!" After our short chat with the doctor, the nurses came in and began preparing my bed, releasing the breaks and rolling up the side bar to keep me from rolling out they were about to take me down to the operating room. Dawn gave me a kiss and I felt the bed begin to roll.

Dawn wouldn't see me again for the next ten hours, and I felt bad for her because I knew she was worried. I was getting a little anxious again while the nurses pushed me down the hallway.

They relaxed me by explaining all of the things I would see when we entered the operating room. Eventually we went through a set of doors and there we were, in a bright, chilly, sterile room surrounded by machines of all shapes and sizes, some beeping and others with tubes coming out of them.

I could see tables on wheels holding trays of shiny stainless steel tools, which were a little intimidating. The people who would be working on me all welcomed me into the room.

They were all covered up with surgical uniforms, even their heads and faces were covered, so all I could see was their eyes. But they were all very nice to me and did their best to assure me everything would be okay.

The nurses rolled my bed over to the thin operating table and helped me scoot onto it, placing my arms on the flaps on each side. I laid my head back onto the pillow and took a deep breath—"here we go," I said under my breath.

I said a little prayer to God, asking him to help me through this so I could see my wife and kids again. The anesthetist put a plastic breathing mask onto my face and said, "Ok, Sonny, we are going to be putting..." And I was out.

This procedure would actually be the first of two surgeries I would have spread across the span of one week. This time they implanted an intracranial electrode grid, which is the placement of electrodes, referred to as intracranial strip or grid electrodes directly onto the brain surface or depth electrodes deeper into the brain tissue.

The electrodes allowed my doctor to precisely map out the areas of my brain causing my seizures as well as the critical areas of my brain that controlled my speech and movement, which she wanted to avoid during the second procedure, when she would be removing the parts of my brain responsible for the seizures.

By identifying the areas of my brain that needed to be removed versus those that needed to be saved, my doctor was able to improve my chances of avoiding any serious neurological effects as well as not having any more seizures.

The actual grid was a clear flexible material impregnated with hundreds of tiny little sensors, (photos on my site) each covered with circular labels to identify each electrode. My doctor hoped the grid would map out where my seizures had been coming from, something the EEG just couldn't show her.

After 10 hours installing the grid, my first procedure was done and I was wheeled down to the intensive care unit. I was a little disoriented and uncomfortable when I woke up from the anesthesia, but the nurses quickly took care of that by giving me extra pain medication. My mother had shown up by this time, too, so she and Dawn were there at my bedside to comfort me.

After that first day, I started eating—endlessly! And I was also surprisingly very happy again, but maybe it was the pain meds? I started getting to know my nurses over time; there were a couple of crabby ones and some pretty humorous ones, too, which made the time go by much easier for me.

In general, though, I'd have to say that most of them were nice. The ones I liked best, though, were the ones who were very mothering, no matter what age I was. Those were the best.

Now that the grid was in place and I had recovered from the procedure, the next thing I had to do was have an actual seizure—never thought the day would come that I would actually want to have a seizure!

Dawn was almost always at my side and we had a room all to ourselves most of the time. I cannot stress highly enough to anyone listening to this how important it is for anyone looking at surgery to have the support of a loved one next to you before, during, and after surgery. I know for a fact that I could not have done it without my dear wife.

I know that at times, sometimes for hours on end, this experience was very stressful on her, worrying about me during my surgeries. I was really glad to have my mother there to sit with her so they could support each other as they worried.

One night they found out the hospital provided an area for family members to stay, so my mother filled in for

Dawn at my bedside while Dawn broke away to steal an evening of some much-needed rest.

Each day the specialists dropped my seizure medications lower and lower in order to trigger a seizure so they could precisely locate the source. It took me a whole week before I was able to give them one while the grid was in place.

So at 11pm I gave them 5 quick seizures within 45 minutes.

So the next day after meeting with all of the other specialists, my doctor informed me that she would meet me in surgery at 5:00 AM the next morning. Then, the next morning I was prepped and wheeled into the operating room for my second surgery. Dawn and my mother took their positions, waiting patiently.

This time my doctor performed what is known as a temporal lobectomy on the left side on my brain.

The surgery went smoothly, thank goodness, and we were all surprised when they explained the removed tissue. The tissue was actually stuck to the side of my skull, they said. She removed one hippocampus in the left Temporal Lobe.

I came out of anesthetic okay and ended up being in bed for just under two weeks after this surgery, which really seemed to wear me down. I noticed immediately that it was hard for me to think of words to express myself, making talking or asking for the things I needed, a real struggle for me.

A few days later a nurse took me outside for a nice, gentle walk on a warm sunny day, but my balance was off and I went only about 30 feet before feeling completely exhausted. In a tender way, she pushed me to go a little further. I thought it was wonderful just being outside, feeling the sun on my face again.

## Making our way home

Two days after my walk, my doctor felt I was strong enough to go home, so Dawn and I prepared ourselves for the long drive home.

Dawn brought a couple of really nice, soft pillows so I could lean my head on the door without bumping the staples I still had in my skull. It felt good to finally be back home, but shortly after arriving I noticed I was having trouble balancing, I felt very weak, and I had lost 30 lbs.

During my recovery I was given steroid medications around the clock for several weeks in order to fight off infection and inflammation. In terms of seizure medication, my specialist decided not to change the dosage right away. She wanted to do it very gradually over time, so we cut it down 25% at the 12-month mark and another 25% at the 18-month mark, and we would see how it goes after that.

Unfortunately, I had to stop using pain medications pretty quickly due to unwanted side effects and switched over to Tylenol, instead. My mother came up to the house to help watch the kids and stay by my side during this time, giving Dawn another much-needed break.

Because I had been so worried before the surgery about how we were all going to manage while I was laid up, it was a pleasant surprise to see my family all pitching in, even the little ones, to make things work.

I could not sleep in my bedroom for over three weeks. Instead, I rested on a new recliner Dawn and I had purchased a month before the surgery. It was okay, though, because this allowed me to interact with my family, watch television, and adjust the angle of my legs and my back.

During the day I looked out the large living room windows next to me, watching the big, strong oak trees sway back and forth on windy days while squirrels hopped effortlessly from branch to branch. Our two acres were very relaxing to watch, but in the back of my mind I was wishing I could get out there and mow the lawn and take care of the landscaping the way I used to.

"Oh well…" I thought to myself, taking a deep breath and closing my eyes as I let my head fall back gently into the pillow.

Interestingly, I was watching very little TV because I could not think fast enough to take it all in. I could tell I was getting tired when I would begin to see flickering on the screen. It was a lot like the kind you see while watching old fashioned black and white films.

The doctor said my brain was still exerting a lot of energy trying to heal, so it got tired easily. At 44 years old, I felt like a baby needing to take a noontime nap before getting up to trying again.

Three months later I was scheduled to see my doctor again for a follow up appointment, which went well. I was impatient and hated the 10 lbs. lifting limit she imposed on me. My speech was still far off from the way it was before the surgery, so I began seeing a speech therapist, which proved to be more difficult than I expected.

For example, my therapist gave me one minute to tell her as many words I could think of starting with the letter "s," and no matter how hard I tried, I could only come up with one measly word. It was so frustrating.

My brain felt so out of control. (Compare this to a more recent visit, on January 6th, 2015, when she asked me to do it again: I did so well she stopped me midway!)

My family continued to support me throughout my recovery, and I think it brought us all closer because it was a chance for us to come together to overcome a challenge. I got a kick out of my girls assisting me with my memory homework—a direct contrast to the days when I helped them with their homework!

We had pictures of items we see all the time, such as dog, car, wreath, and pencil that were surprisingly all very difficult for me. I also had to read small stories about a paragraph in length and then try to explain what I had just read.

I just didn't do well at all. My therapist explained that my memory was trying to find words where they had always been stored, but now it had to relearn the words and find them in their new locations.

She said repetition helps with this. We also learned from her that I could remember a small list of things as long as they were told to me slowly, with a pause in between, giving my brain time to encode each word into its new location from which it could retrieve them again, later. We tried this and it did make a difference.

We noticed a few side effects from the surgery. First of all, I wasn't depressed anymore, and I didn't get upset about things the way I used to. Even my friends and family told me I seemed more confident, happy, and relaxed.

And there were other effects, such as seeing things to the left that weren't there, almost like hallucinating, I even changed the type of guitar I was making and playing from a regular six-string to a four-string bass with interest of piano.

In addition, noticed I no longer liked to have noise in the background the way I used to, such as playing a television or radio its difficult keeping focus. More often now I like peace and quiet.

September of 2013 marked my 18th month since surgery, and I couldn't believe I had gone a whole year and a half without having a single aura or seizure!!! I had another follow up appointment with my specialist, during which we discussed how I was doing with my speech and memory.

I wasn't expecting anything exciting, but boy was I mistaking! While finishing our appointment my specialist said, "Hey Sonny, one more thing…". "How would you like to start driving?" What? Nah… really?

Was she really serious? She said she was serious and I had the option once again, to get my license. This was the moment I realized, how far we'd come, how much I had really achieved. My life was starting to change for the better and I liked the man I was becoming.

Two months later, I was up in Detroit Lakes preparing to take my driver's test (again). I was both confident and nervous at the same time, but my daughter Riley, then only 10-years- old, had no doubt I would pass.

Out of nowhere, my neighbor, Pam, a wonderful friend who is now the mother-in-law of my oldest stepdaughter, called me up one day and said, "Hey, Sonny, how about if I swing by to pick you up so we can go take your drivers permit test?

I passed that, then two months later Pam and I went into town and as Riley predicted I passed the on the road test!

So the first thing I did that afternoon was pickup Riley at school. What a liberating feeling to finally be able to do something so simple like that.

She immediately recognized the car and came running to it, but was surprised to see who was in it. She jumped into the passenger seat and leaned over to give me a big hug and kiss. And then, in true Riley style, she told me nonchalantly, "I knew you could do it, dad."

Since we had been just recently purchased a new car for Kelsey, to commute to college through the dangerously winter weather in Fargo, I was left driving her old car, the Taurus, which was in bad need of repair.

Winter was just around the corner, and word about the car situation got back to my sister in California, who without my knowledge, shopped online and bought me a shiny blue late model Jeep Patriot from a dealer nearby Detroit Lakes, so I could have it maintained there as needed. She and my mother planned a Christmas visit with us, Chera and Mustafa flying over and mom and her husband, Jim, driving up. The day they arrived it was windy and bitter cold with three feet of snow on the ground and still snowing. They invited us over to the hotel for a dinner overlooking the lake from inside the cozy restaurant.

Little did I know, they had gone and picked up the Jeep and set it up under the eve of the hotel entrance with a big red bow and gift tag on the hood. It was dark by the time we pulled in, and, of course, I was focusing on the people standing outside, not looking for a blue Jeep, so I got out of my wife's van and walked within a few feet right passed the front bumper of the Jeep that had the gift tag saying

"SONNY" in big bold red letters.

I saw my sister standing outside the hotel door and walked up to give her a hug. Before I let go, she pointed over my shoulder with a smile and told me to turn around. I didn't know what she wanted me to look at, but when I turned around and saw the Jeep with the big red bow on it, I figured out what was going on and squeezed her again. Then I found Mustafa and gave him a big hug and thanked him.

I jumped in the Jeep and took Riley and Kaleigh for a quick drive through the deep snow and then back to the hotel to have dinner. Chera and Mustafa said they were very proud of me for turning into such a wonder father and husband despite all of the challenges I faced growing up with my epilepsy.

They wanted me to have something safe to drive that I could be proud of, something that was all mine, free and clear. We had a wonderful time together that night around the large table.

Even though it had been snowing all night long and continued to snow the next morning, we all piled into the Jeep so I could give them a tour of Detroit Lakes. It was weird… this was the first time I wasn't the passenger with my sister, Mustafa, mom, and Jim.

Thanks to having a dependable vehicle, I was able to get a good job, the one I still have to this day.

## Making a difference

It gives my life value just knowing that all of my years of suffering, were not in vain. Because I know that I can share my story with other families and give them hope.

In January 2014 I was invited to tell my story at the monthly parents meeting of the EFMN (Epilepsy Foundation of Minnesota). I learned so much from the other parents in terms of raising children with epilepsy—I told them they were all heroes.

In June that same year, I was thrilled to see that my story had been published in the E F's Magazine. And two months after that, on August 7th, 2014, I was invited to tell my story at the EFMN's "Stroll for Epilepsy," event, which was a walk to benefit families in North Dakota and Minnesota with epilepsy.

I told my story to over 300 people in the North Dakota State University's Fargo Dome that night. What a wonderful evening that was.

In preparation, I was scared at the thought of speaking in front of so many people, but the love and support I felt from everyone who was there gave me the courage to follow through with it.

I was so glad I made the decision to do it in the end. I encouraged every one of the families there to never give up, no matter how many barriers they run into or how depressed they become.

They need to make tough decisions that will help them overcome their seizures, just like I did. They need to know their lives have value and to just keep pressing forward.

Another way of telling my story to others included writing a poem. The Epilepsy Foundation encourages people to share their personal experiences by writing and submitting poems or stories about their lives with epilepsy and then the foundation chooses the best ones to print in its annual

"Epilogues" book.

With the exception of elementary school almost 40 years ago, I don't think I've ever written any poems before, but I was inspired by the work of the Epilepsy Foundation and decided to write one called "Decisions," which I am very proud to say made it onto the first page of the 2015 Epilogues book! That was a real validation for me that I have made it.

The last milestone of my story, as of the time of writing this book, at least, was a relatively simple one. On January 6$^{th}$, 2015 I went to see my specialist again. We hadn't seen each other for a year and a half. This time I told her that I would be in charge of our appointment.

She smiled, nodding her head. I told her a bit, about all that had happened since our last meeting and then held out my hand with a paper in it, saying, "Read this!" She started reading the small story I had written in the Epilepsy Foundation Magazine, and I saw a small tear run down her cheek, so I stood up and gave her a hug.

I want this story to motivate people… to motivate those who have put their lives on hold, just going through the day-to-day motions of existence without achieving life goals.

I want those individuals and their families to take action to get the help they need for their epilepsy, their depression, and whatever other challenges they are facing. I want them to move their lives forward.

I was blessed with a caring family who supported me throughout all of it, my mother and sister and their husbands, Dawn's brothers and parents, and (in order of birth) my children, step kids Kelsey, Jared, and Kaleigh, and the youngest, my daughter, Riley.

And, of course, my high school sweetheart and the greatest partner in life I could ever ask for, my wife, Dawn.

## Decisions

When we have epilepsy, all of us know
Losing self-dignity, will not always show

My education was difficult, confusing at times
But family and friends are a blessing of mine

In 2011, my decisions were made
Stability in life would be a great trade

I finally decided to go out on a limb
God opened the door and let me come in

Early in my life, were difficult years
Even at times, caused me tears

I'm now on a mission to open your eyes
Do not give up, you may be surprised!

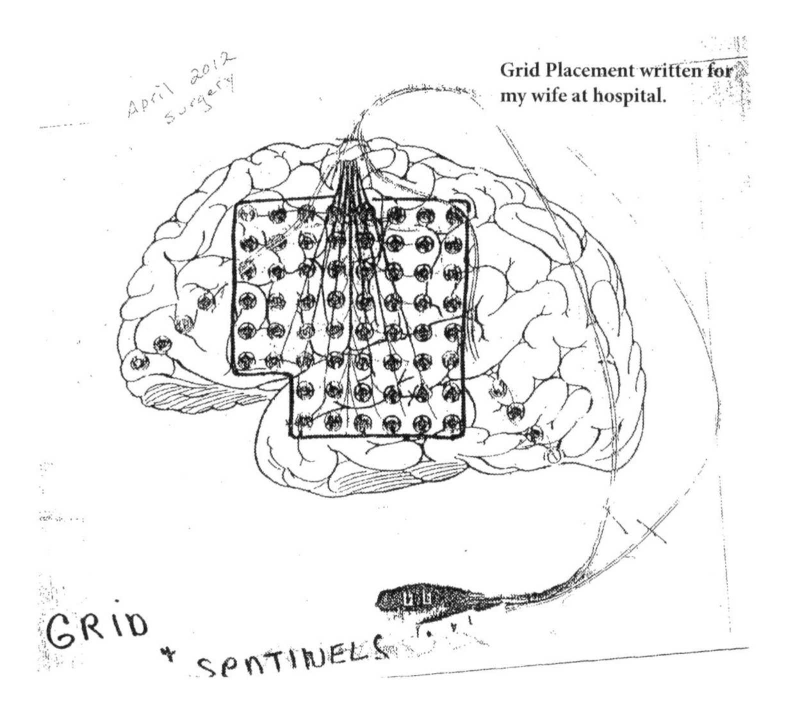
Grid Placement written for
my wife at hospital.
April 2012
Surgery
GRID
+ SENTINELS

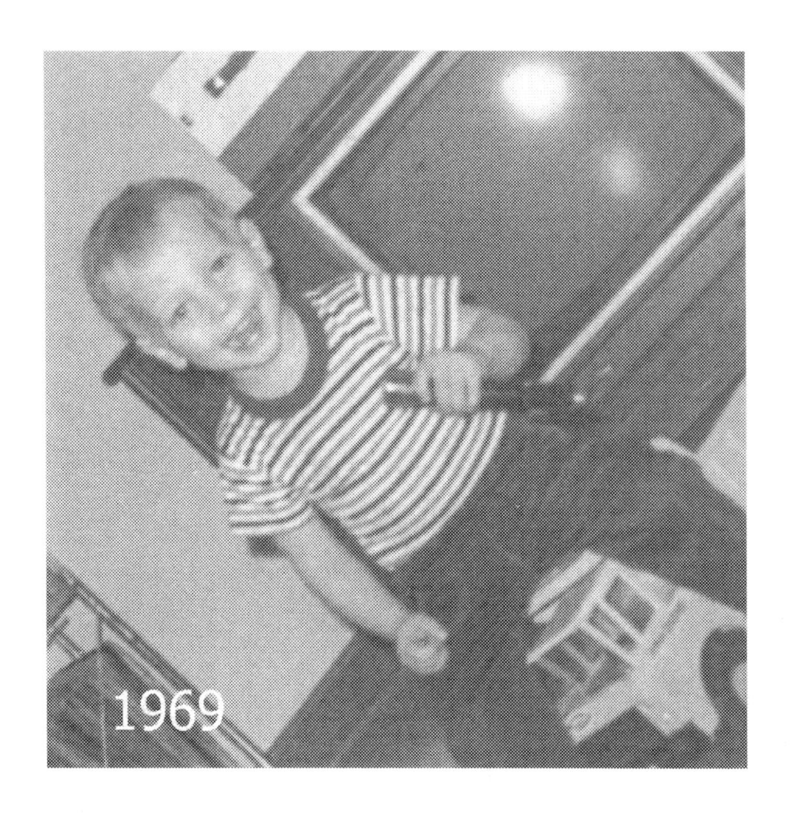
1969

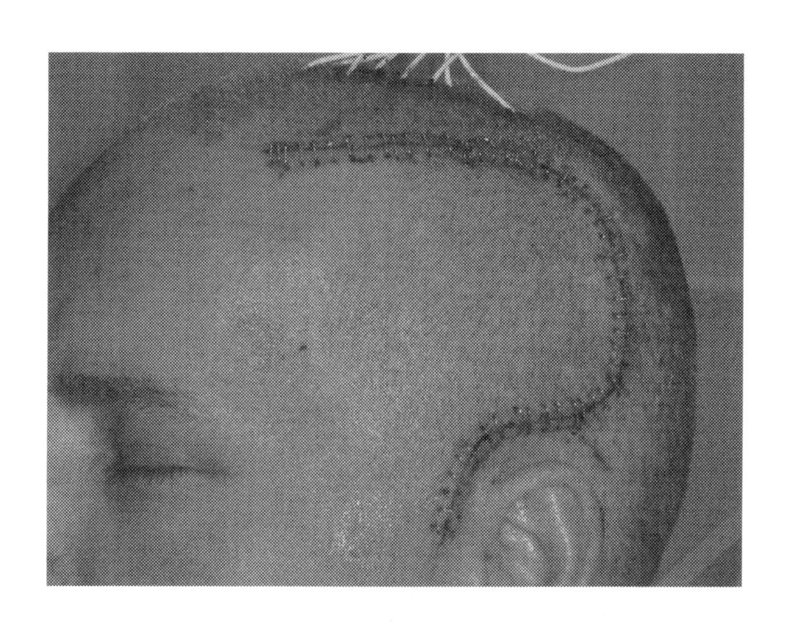

Printed in the United States
By Bookmasters